AMERICAN VALUES AND FREEDOMS

GOVERNMENTAL CHECKS AND BALANCES

by DUCHESS HARRIS, JD, PHD

Essential Library

An Imprint of Abdo Publishing | abdopublishing.com

YA
320.47
HAR

ABDOPUBLISHING.COM

Published by Abdo Publishing, a division of ABDO, PO Box 398166, Minneapolis, Minnesota 55439. Copyright © 2018 by Abdo Consulting Group, Inc. International copyrights reserved in all countries. No part of this book may be reproduced in any form without written permission from the publisher. Essential Library™ is a trademark and logo of Abdo Publishing.

Printed in the United States of America, North Mankato, Minnesota
102017
012018

THIS BOOK CONTAINS RECYCLED MATERIALS

Interior Photos: Universal Images Group/Getty Images, 4; Theodore R. Davis/Library of Congress, 9; Frank Duenzl/picture-alliance/dpa/AP Images, 14; Library of Congress, 19; Reed Saxon/AP Images, 20; Evan Vucci/AP Images, 24, 90–91; Louis Buller/AP Images, 26–27; AP Images, 29, 56, 63, 76, 96; John Duricka/AP Images, 33; Sean Pavone Photo/iStockphoto, 36–37; Jacquelyn Martin/AP Images, 39; Bill Clark/CQ Roll Call/AP Images, 42; Ron Sachs/picture-alliance/dpa/AP Images, 43; Olivier Douliery/picture-alliance/dpa/AP Images, 46; iStockphoto, 48–49; Cheriss May/Sipa USA/AP Images, 51; Rex Features/AP Images, 58; Maryann Groves/North Wind Picture Archives, 65; Susan Walsh/AP Images, 68; North Wind Picture Archives, 70; John Bazemore/AP Images, 74; Alex Brandon/AP Images, 77; Lana Harris/AP Images, 80; J. Scott Applewhite/AP Images, 87

Editor: Patrick Donnelly
Series Designer: Becky Daum
Contributor: Don Nardo

Publisher's Cataloging-in-Publication Data

Names: Harris, Duchess, author.
Title: Governmental checks and balances / by Duchess Harris.
Description: Minneapolis, Minnesota : Abdo Publishing, 2018. | Series: American values and freedoms | Online resources and index.
Identifiers: LCCN 2017946726 | ISBN 9781532113017 (lib.bdg.) | ISBN 9781532151897 (ebook)
Subjects: LCSH: Separation of powers–Juvenile literature. | United States–Juvenile literature. | Politics and government–Juvenile literature. | Constitutional law–United States–Juvenile literature.
Classification: DDC 320.47304–dc23
LC record available at https://lccn.loc.gov/2017946726

CONTENTS

CHAPTER 1

CONGRESS VERSUS ANDREW JOHNSON

February 24, 1868, was not a good day for Andrew Johnson, the seventeenth president of the United States. As the day began, he knew well that many members of Congress were angry with him. Most were Republicans, members of the party of his predecessor, Abraham Lincoln. A Democrat, Johnson had served as Lincoln's vice president. Then, after Lincoln's assassination in April 1865, Johnson had assumed the office of president.

Andrew Johnson was the first US president to face impeachment.

ANGRY CONGRESSIONAL REPUBLICANS

Johnson knew one major reason why the Republicans disliked him: he frequently used the presidential veto. Approximately 80 years earlier, the US founders had created the veto. It was part of the US Constitution. In essence, that document was the detailed blueprint they had crafted for the national government. They intended the veto to be a tool used by the president to check, or limit, Congress's powers. That would prevent the lawmakers in Congress from dominating the government. Johnson had taken full advantage of his veto power. Between 1866 and 1868, he had rejected many bills Congress had passed.

There was something even more upsetting for the Republicans in Congress, Johnson realized. It was his handling of the Tenure of Office Act. Congress had recently passed it in an attempt to reduce presidential authority. It kept Johnson from removing officeholders Congress had appointed. The president vetoed the law in March 1867. Fuming over that move, however, congressional Republicans utilized a constitutional check of their own. If Congress can muster enough votes, it can override, or reverse, a presidential veto.

After Congress restored the Tenure of Office Act, Johnson attacked it again. This time, he fired Secretary of War Edwin Stanton, whom Congress had earlier approved. The president tried to replace Stanton with General Ulysses S. Grant. When both Stanton and Congress strongly objected, however, Grant changed his mind. Then Johnson appointed another general, Lorenzo Thomas, to the post. Hearing this, Stanton said he would not step down. He locked himself in his office and refused to come out.

THE TENURE OF OFFICE ACT

President Johnson's contempt for the Tenure of Office Act was the chief reason Congress impeached him. The legislature's members passed it on March 2, 1867. It forbade the president from getting rid of officials appointed by the Senate without its permission. Congress's intent was to limit Johnson's ability to interfere with its plans. In particular, it did not want the president to fire Secretary of War Edwin M. Stanton. (As did many Republicans, Stanton favored harsh treatment of the South after the Civil War.) In 1887, federal judges found the Tenure of Office Act to be unconstitutional, and it was eliminated.

JOHNSON IS IMPEACHED

The defiant stands made by Johnson and Stanton over the Tenure of Office Act further angered congressional Republicans. They decided to exercise another check the Constitution had granted Congress. Called impeachment, it charges the president with committing a crime. Other high-placed officials can also be similarly charged. Members of the House of Representatives take a vote. If a majority of them vote yes, the president is impeached, or officially charged.

Johnson realized that if he was impeached, he would have to face a trial in the Senate. Several House members would become the impeachment managers. They would prosecute the case against him. Meanwhile, the senators would hear the evidence presented by the prosecutors and Johnson's own attorneys. The chief justice of the Supreme Court would oversee the trial. After all the evidence had been presented, the senators would vote. They might acquit Johnson, finding him innocent. Or they could convict him, finding him guilty. A conviction would mean his removal from office.

Soon after Secretary Stanton locked himself in his office, the impeachment process began. On February 24, 1868, the House of Representatives took its initial vote. The tally was not in Johnson's favor. The congressmen had elected to impeach him by a vote of 126 to 47. Seventeen members chose not to vote, which was their right.[1]

The next day, the House impeachment managers gathered. They were led by Pennsylvania's Thaddeus Stevens, perhaps

Johnson's staunchest enemy in the House. The men were expected to walk from the House chamber to the Senate chamber, where they would deliver the official news that the president had been impeached.

Stevens was ill and too weak to walk that far unaided, however, so his assistants carried him in an armchair to the Senate chamber's door. Using all his strength, Stevens stood up and rested his weight on a cane. Followed by the other impeachment managers, he limped inside and suddenly spoke in a booming voice. "We appear before you," he said, "and in the name of the House of Representatives and all the people of the United States, [we] do impeach Andrew Johnson."[2]

WAS JOHNSON TOO LENIENT TOWARD THE SOUTH?

One reason many congressional Republicans disliked Johnson was his policy toward the South. A Democrat, he had succeeded Abraham Lincoln, a Republican. Johnson desired to more or less implement Lincoln's plans following the recent Civil War when overseeing Reconstruction, or the reunification of the North and the South. Those plans called for a lenient treatment of the Southern states, whose secession triggered the war. He faced objection from Thaddeus Stevens and other Republican leaders. They wanted the South to be punished severely for leaving and fighting the Union. They also feared that former enslaved people would be treated unfairly by Southerners. But each time the Republicans passed a law that treated the South harshly, Johnson vetoed it.

A SPEEDY TRIAL

On March 7, 1868, a Senate messenger delivered a summons, or request to appear in court, to President Johnson. It listed the 11 crimes Congress had charged him with. Of the two most serious charges, one claimed the president's firing of Secretary Stanton had violated the Tenure of Office Act. The second grave charge said that Johnson had slandered Congress, or falsely spoken ill of it. Having read all the charges, Johnson turned to his head lawyer, Henry Stanbery, who told the president he did not have to appear physically at the trial. So Johnson stayed home throughout the proceedings. He kept up with what was happening through his lawyers and newspaper reports.

The trial began in the Senate soon afterward, on March 13. Johnson's attorneys requested that the presiding judge give them 40 days to prepare the case properly. The prosecution argued against that motion, however. Impeachment manager Benjamin Butler insisted that the trial proceed right away.

As he followed the trial, Johnson often became agitated or angry. The prosecutors sometimes called him unflattering names, and many predicted a quick defeat for the president. Johnson fought back as best he could and always proclaimed his innocence. He would never "do a dishonorable act contrary to law," he told one of his lawyers. He would rather "suffer my right arm torn from its socket," he added.[3]

THE CONSTITUTION'S MAJESTIC POWERS

In the weeks that followed, the prosecution called 25 witnesses to testify against the president. The defense, meanwhile, called 16 witnesses who spoke highly of Johnson. Finally, on May 16, 1868, it was time for the senators to cast their ballots. How they voted would determine whether the man in the White House would stay there or be thrown out.

MIXED REACTIONS TO JOHNSON'S ACQUITTAL

The reactions to Johnson's acquittal were, not surprisingly, mixed. Some Americans shared Thaddeus Stevens's disappointment and anger. Witnesses described how he waved his arms in the air and bellowed, "The country is going to the devil!"[5] A Florida Republican echoed this sentiment. "It is with sadness we learn that the greatest traitor of the century is acquitted," he wrote. "May God save our country."[6] Large numbers of Americans were elated over the news of the acquittal, however. A Georgia man, Henry S. Fitch, wrote to Johnson, saying, "the vote on impeachment has sent a thrill of joy throughout the state. [The] people are with you heart and soul."[7] On May 17, 1868, Benjamin Rush, an American living in Paris, also sent joyous tidings. "Permit me," Rush began, "to mingle my heartfelt congratulations with those of tens of thousands of my fellow citizens who are doubtless at this moment offering you theirs. . . . [The] unparalleled outrage attempted to be perpetrated upon you [will] blacken our history to the end of time."[8]

In a dramatic, memorable scene, one by one the senators cast their votes. The final tally was 35 votes of "yes," to convict Johnson, and 19 votes of "no," to acquit him. A majority of senators had voted against him, but it was not enough for a guilty verdict. According to another of the Constitution's checks and balances, conviction required a two-thirds majority. Fifty-four senators had voted, and two-thirds of 54 is 36. Therefore Johnson had escaped conviction by a single vote.[4]

Another factor had saved the president:

a few Republicans had voted to acquit. One of them, Iowa's James Grimes, later said that the trial had disturbed him. In his view, it threatened to "destroy the harmonious working of the Constitution." He could not do that, he said, "for the sake of getting rid of an unacceptable president."[9]

In this classic political showdown from American history, therefore, three important constitutional checks played their parts. First, President Johnson checked Congress's power with his many vetoes. Then, Congress tried to limit the executive's power by impeaching him. Finally, Congress's power was checked again by the need for two-thirds of the senators to vote for conviction. In the end, both sides had to bow to the Constitution's powers.

DISCUSSION STARTERS

- Do you agree with the stand Andrew Johnson took on the Tenure of Office Act? Why or why not?

- In your view, was locking himself in his office the best way for Edwin Stanton to handle the situation? Why or why not?

- Why do you think President Johnson preferred treating the defeated Southern states leniently? Do you feel that policy would have been effective? Why or why not?

CHAPTER 2

CREATING CHECKS AND BALANCES

On January 27, 2017, US president Donald Trump issued a presidential order. It banned people from seven Middle Eastern and African nations from traveling to the United States. He claimed he was trying to guard against terrorists entering the country from those nations. One week later, a federal judge in Seattle, Washington, halted Trump's travel ban. The judge said the president's order was unconstitutional. That is, it did not uphold the principles of the US Constitution, the blueprint for the US government.

Protesters at San Diego International Airport rally against a proposed travel ban in January 2017.

FOUR JUDGES CHECK THE PRESIDENT'S POWER

The travel ban that President Donald Trump proposed in early 2017 focused on seven mostly Muslim countries: Iran, Iraq, Yemen, Syria, Libya, Somalia, and Sudan. But US District Court judge James Robart temporarily suspended the ban. Robart said it failed to uphold the Constitution. The president's lawyers protested, but a three-judge panel upheld the suspension. This was a potent example of the judicial branch checking the executive branch.

This incident showed one of the Constitution's several checks and balances in action. The judge checked the president's power, meaning he blocked or limited it. In a sense, Trump's order had caused an imbalance in governmental powers. The judge's check sought to bring them back into balance.

The Constitution's checks and balances remain a tribute to the wisdom of the founders. Those creators of the US political system fashioned them 230 years before Trump issued his travel ban. In May 1787, representatives from 12 of the 13 original American colonies met in Philadelphia. Rhode Island, the missing colony, joined the others a few months later. These Founding Fathers, or founders for short, had a challenging mission: to create a constitution for the national government of their recently established nation. Only 11 years earlier, in

1776, they had declared their independence from Britain. In so doing, they had created the United States of America.

THE THREE GOVERNMENTAL BRANCHES

Because the meeting in Philadelphia was held to draft a US constitution, it became known as the Constitutional Convention. The founders intended the document to be a detailed plan for the new national government. It provided for a chief executive called the president, who would be in charge of the government's executive branch. Its task would be to run the government on a daily and yearly basis.

The new constitution also provided for a legislature, or lawmaking body, which made up the government's legislative branch. It was divided into two houses, or groups of lawmakers. One was the Senate. Its members were initially chosen by the state legislatures. The other was the House of Representatives. Its members are elected directly by the residents of each state.

The third branch the founders fashioned was the judiciary, made up of courts presided over by judges. A few of those individuals, called justices, would sit on the nation's highest, most powerful court—the Supreme Court. The Constitution also allowed Congress to create some lower federal courts as needed.

This new system of government was clearly ingenious and potentially effective. It did have certain initial weaknesses, however. Perhaps the most glaring was a lack of diversity. At the time, all members of the three governmental branches were white men. There were no women. Nor were there any black people or members of other minorities. As history would show, this weakness would be addressed and corrected in later generations.

THE THREAT OF TYRANNY

The Constitution's framers, or creators, gave each of the three branches specific powers. They also made sure that the branches and their powers were clearly separate. It was important, for example, for the president not to have legislative powers. Similarly, the legislature should not have the powers of court judges. This concept became known as the separation of powers.

As founder and framer James Madison put it, "The legislative, executive, and judiciary departments ought to be separate and distinct." Making the governmental branches separate, he said, was vital. It would keep any one branch from accumulating too much power. If a president, for

James Madison was the fourth president of the United States and a key framer of the Constitution.

example, did possess too much authority, he might become a dictator. Madison warned against "the accumulation of all powers legislative, executive, and judiciary in the same hands." Such a situation would be "the very definition of tyranny."[2]

The separation of powers was plainly an important safeguard against a tyrannical government. Several of the framers remained worried, however. Keeping one branch from using another branch's powers was certainly a step in the right direction, they said. Yet another danger loomed.

JUDICIAL CHECKS

On February 9, 2017, a three-judge panel upheld Judge James Robart's February 3 suspension of President Donald Trump's widely controversial travel ban. In this example of a judiciary check on the president, the three judges agreed on several points. First, they said, there was no urgent need for the travel ban to be immediately instated. Second, officials in some states had shown that a number of their residents would be harmed by the ban. Also, Trump had argued that the ban was required to maintain national security. Yet the judges countered that claim. There was "no evidence," they said, "that any alien from any of the countries named in the [ban] has perpetrated a terrorist attack in the United States." In addition, the judges felt the travel ban discriminated against Muslims. "It targets Muslim-majority nations," they stated. As a result, the ban "constitutes religious discrimination." Muslim groups across the United States came out in favor of the judges' ruling. Farhana Khera, executive director of the civil rights group Muslim Advocate, stated that this check on the president's power "upheld long-treasured American values of the rule of law and liberty and equality for all, regardless of religion."[3]

A protester at Los Angeles International Airport shows support for Judge James Robart's decision to suspend President Donald Trump's controversial travel ban.

What if one branch amassed an unusually large amount of its own powers? Moreover, what if those powers overshadowed the other two branches' authority? If that happened, the framers reasoned, the strongest branch might abuse its powers. That could very well allow a government official to do undemocratic things.

THE ARGUMENT FOR CHECKS AND BALANCES

To avoid that threat to the American people, the framers considered adding another safeguard to the Constitution. It consisted of the various checks and balances. These special powers were granted to each governmental branch. They were designed to counteract certain powers held by the other two branches. Thus, if one branch exercised too much power, another branch could curb that authority to some degree. The result would be a more balanced, fairer government. Thanks to the checks and balances, the system would not likely lapse into tyranny.

Madison made the strongest argument for adding the checks and balances. He later explained his position in writing in an essay titled "The Federalist No. 51." It was one of 85 articles collectively called the Federalist Papers. Madison and two other framers—Alexander Hamilton and John Jay—wrote

MADISON ON LEGISLATIVE CHECKS

James Madison outlined most of his arguments for creating checks and balances in the Federalist No. 51. One important example he cited there was choosing the proper structure for the national legislature. After all, he said, Congress makes the laws and can change the Constitution. It was therefore essential, he stated, that Congress not be allowed to amass too much power. This is why the founders decided to create two congressional houses—the Senate and the House of Representatives. Madison said they should not only be two in number and separate. They should also have their members chosen by "different modes of election and different principles of action."[4] Following this principle, the founders chose to have House members elected by the people. In contrast, senators were originally elected by members of the state legislatures. In 1913, the Seventeenth Amendment to the Constitution altered this. Ever since, senators have been directly elected by the people. Madison made sure that these legislative checks and balances became part of the government's basic structure.

them soon after the convention ended. The essays were published and read widely throughout the 13 colonies. Each explained in detail why the framers had added a certain feature to the Constitution. The founders hoped the essays would convince the states' leaders to ratify the document. A number of those leaders were reluctant at first to ratify. This was mainly because of the earlier US governing system, the short-lived Articles of Confederation. In it, the states had more authority, and the federal government had less authority, than in the new system.

In the Federalist No. 51, Madison wrote about one of the framers' biggest worries. It was, he said, "the gradual concentration of the several powers in the same department," or branch. That is, one governmental branch should not be allowed to overpower the other two branches. To guard against this tendency, "ambition must be made to counter ambition." That is, the power of one branch must counter, or limit, the power of another branch.[5]

It was only natural that presidents, congressmen, and judges would have personal ambitions to wield power, Madison wrote. They are, after all, only human. "If men were angels," he joked, "no government would be necessary." If angels ran a country, he added, no "controls on government would be necessary." Clearly, however, humans are not angels, Madison stated. So the government must be forced "to control itself."[6]

LAYERS OF SAFEGUARDS

The governmental "controls" Madison mentioned were the checks and balances. These safeguards later repeatedly showed themselves to be both necessary and effective. One of the most often used has been the veto, which allows a president to stop enactment of a questionable law. Of course,

President George W. Bush had one of his vetoes overridden by Congress in 2007.

it is possible for a president to overuse or otherwise abuse the veto power. Aware of this potential, the framers wisely provided another check to counter the veto. It is the congressional override. A two-thirds vote of both houses of Congress overrides, or cancels out, a veto.

The veto override has been used a number of times since the founders created it. A clear-cut example occurred in 2007 after President George W. Bush vetoed the Water Resources Development Act. It provided for scientific studies to investigate ways to control floods. Bush thought it was too costly and vetoed it, but most members of Congress felt his stance was misguided. One lawmaker called it an "irresponsible veto." Soon afterward, the Senate and House overrode it.[7]

After the override, the bill became law. Even if it had been a bad law all along, however, the system could still have stopped it. This is thanks to still another check, which the Supreme Court developed in practice not long after the Constitution was ratified. It is that court's ability to declare any law unconstitutional. In this way, the US founders, along with the initial high court justices, cleverly created layers of checks and balances. More than two centuries later, they continue to help the American people avoid tyrannical government.

DISCUSSION STARTERS

- In your view, is the separation of powers system created by the founders fairer and more effective than a system in which the president has legislative powers? Why or why not?

- Madison and his colleagues wrote the Federalist Papers to tell the American people why the founders had included various ideas in the Constitution. Would publishing essays in that manner be an effective way for leaders to convey ideas to the people today? Why or why not? If not, what other ways might be more effective?

- The founders designated a two-thirds, or 67 percent, majority of lawmakers to override a veto. Why do you think they chose that proportion? Why do you think they did not make it, say, 55 percent or 90 percent?

CHAPTER 3

CONGRESS CHECKS THE PRESIDENT

original and best listings magazine

Is love
poetry
dead?
In Saturday

NEWSPAPER OF THE YEAR   WEEKEND EDITION

Plus: why
Keegan is
not the man
for the job
By David Lacey

ney

FT

FINANCIAL TIMES
FEBRUARY 13/FEBRUARY 14 1999

uardian

linton – humbled,
US president

s for
n
al

THE E

British newspapers display reactions to the US Senate's acquittal of President Bill Clinton on charges of perjury and obstruction of justice.

Among the many checks and balances the founders created, perhaps the best known are some of those curbing presidential power. In particular, the legislative branch can check the president in several ways. The founders felt this was necessary because the Constitution grants the president numerous powers. There is always a chance that he or she might abuse those powers. So Congress has the authority to try "to hold presidents accountable to the rule of law," scholar Chris Edelson explains. After all, "the president is, unlike a monarch, subject to the rule of law like everyone else."[1]

THE IMPEACHMENT OPTION

The most powerful check Congress can use against the chief executive is impeachment. The House charges a president with a crime, and the Senate holds a trial. If convicted, the president is removed from office. There is also a countercheck to protect the president from an overeager Congress, as conviction requires a large majority of senators to find him or her guilty. "When the President of the United States is tried," the Constitution states, "two thirds of the [Senate's] members" must vote to convict.[2]

To date, no US president has been impeached and convicted. Two were impeached, or charged with wrongdoing, and underwent Senate trials. The first was Andrew Johnson, who managed to escape conviction by a single vote in 1868. The other chief executive who underwent the impeachment process was Bill Clinton. In 1998, the House of Representatives charged him with lying. He initially claimed he had not had a sexual relationship with a White House intern, Monica Lewinsky. But it later came out that he had.

In the Senate trial, the House prosecutors argued that Clinton had covered up the affair. That, they insisted, amounted to obstruction of justice, a serious crime. But a majority of the senators who heard the case disagreed. They felt that the lies involved were not serious enough to call for his removal from office. Like President Johnson, therefore, Clinton was acquitted. Both men served out the remainders of their terms.

While neither Johnson nor Clinton had spotless records, they were impeached mainly for political reasons. Many members of Congress did not like them or their policies and wanted a different president. In another instance, however, impeachment proceedings began because a president actually did commit a serious crime. This was the case of President Richard Nixon.

In June 1972, near the end of Nixon's first term, a burglary occurred in the Watergate Building in Washington, DC. Several Republicans were arrested for trying to steal Democratic Party documents. A few months

Richard M. Nixon waves to his supporters as he boards a helicopter to leave the White House after resigning the presidency.

RICHARD NIXON RESIGNS

On August 8, 1974, President Richard M. Nixon gave his resignation speech on live television. He had decided to quit the presidency because much evidence of his part in the Watergate scandal had emerged. It had become clear that Congress would soon impeach and convict him for that. He did not mention his crimes in the speech, however. Instead, he claimed he was resigning because his base of support in Congress had eroded:

> In all the decisions I have made in my public life, I have always tried to do what was best for the Nation. Throughout the long and difficult period of Watergate, I have felt it was my duty to persevere, to make every possible effort to complete the term of office to which you elected me. In the past few days, however, it has become evident to me that I no longer have a strong enough political base in the Congress to justify continuing that effort. . . . With the disappearance of that base, I now believe that the constitutional purpose has been served, and there is no longer a need for the process to be prolonged.[3]

later, news reporters connected the break-in to members of Nixon's reelection campaign.

As time went on, it appeared that the president was part of a cover-up of the Watergate crime. So in July 1973, many Americans began calling for his impeachment. In the summer of the following year, it became clear that impeachment was about to start in the House. Realizing that eventual conviction was likely, Nixon chose to avoid that disgrace. On August 8, 1974, he became the only US president to resign.

VETO OVERRIDES AND PRESIDENTIAL APPOINTMENTS

Another important check that Congress can use against the executive branch is the power to override a president's veto. Two-thirds of the members of both legislative houses must vote against the veto. Between 1789 and January 2017, Congress overrode 111 presidential vetoes. Andrew Johnson holds the record for the most vetoes canceled out. Of his 29 vetoes, Congress overrode 15. Harry S. Truman and Gerald Ford are tied for second, with 12 overridden vetoes each.[4]

The simple threat of a veto override can promote cooperation between the president and Congress. For example, to put pressure on the president, the legislature can say it has the necessary votes for a veto override. Then, historian Donald A. Ritchie writes, "it is likely the president will make every effort to compromise on the issue."[5]

Congress can also limit a president's authority by rejecting his or her picks for various government positions. The Constitution allows the president to appoint cabinet members. He or she can also choose judges, foreign ambassadors, and other officials. As a check on that power, however, Congress must approve such appointments by a two-thirds vote.

Most often the legislature approves the chief executive's choices. On those occasions when Congress rejects such picks, however, controversy can ensue. In 1987, for instance, President Ronald Reagan nominated Judge Robert Bork for the Supreme Court. A former law professor, Bork had plenty of experience. Nevertheless, some lawmakers objected. They claimed his views on certain topics were too extreme. That made him too biased for the high court. In the end, Congress refused to approve Bork for the position. President Reagan later nominated Judge Anthony Kennedy for the same job, and he was approved.

FOREIGN TREATIES

There is another way Congress can use a refusal of approval to check a president's power. The Constitution says the chief executive can "make treaties, provided two-thirds of the senators present concur."[6] A well-known example of this constitutional check in action happened in 1920. World War I, in which many Americans died, had concluded two years before. President Woodrow Wilson helped to forge the formal agreement that ended hostilities. Called the Treaty of Versailles, many nations signed it in June 1919.

Wilson submitted the treaty to Congress for official approval three months later. Then, in October, he had a massive stroke.

Thereafter he was confined to the White House for the rest of his term. In the meantime, in March 1920 the Senate refused to ratify the Treaty of Versailles. By that time, most Americans blamed Wilson for getting the country into the war. By rejecting the treaty, the Senate sent Wilson the message that the nation should stay out of foreign conflicts.

MAKING WAR

Another possible way Congress can stop a president from getting involved in a war involves money. The executive branch has no power to raise revenue, but Congress does. Raising funds for various government projects, including wars, originates in the House of Representatives. For that reason, it is customary to say that Congress has "the power of the

Judge Robert Bork is sworn in before the Senate Judiciary Committee at his confirmation hearing on September 15, 1987.

GEORGE H. W. BUSH AND THE WAR POWERS ACT

One of the best known examples of the War Powers Act keeping a president's authority in check occurred in 1990. Iraqi dictator Saddam Hussein had recently taken over the tiny neighboring nation of Kuwait. US president George H. W. Bush wanted to send troops to free Kuwait from Saddam's grasp. Bush did not simply invade Iraq, however. He first went to Congress in accordance with the War Powers Act. The legislature passed a resolution approving use of force. Bush's son, who later served as president, also obtained approval from Congress to justify US interventions in Afghanistan and Iraq.

purse." In Ritchie's words, "using the power of the purse, Congress can restrain military action by cutting off funds."[7]

In another related congressional check, only Congress can formally declare war. At times, presidents have found ways to get around that rule. For example, some claim an emergency forces them to send soldiers to fight somewhere. Often Congress agrees this is necessary and allows an undeclared war to proceed. Primary examples of this practice are the Korean War (1950–1953) and the Vietnam War (1954–1975). In both cases, the president ordered the armed forces into action. Also, both conflicts initially seemed necessary to most Americans. But over time they became immensely unpopular. As a result, in 1973 Congress further limited the president's war-making abilities by passing the War Powers Act. It forces the president to consult with Congress before sending troops into combat.

The law has another requirement, scholar Thomas E. Patterson explains. The president must "inform Congress within 48 hours of the reason for the military action." Over time, this and other congressional checks have helped to restrain executive power, he adds. They have forced the president "to keep in mind that Congress is a co-equal branch of the American governing system."[8] Nevertheless, presidents have continued to take military actions—usually limited, yet still lethal—without consulting Congress. One example is President Barack Obama's use of armed drones in Iraq and Syria between 2010 and 2016. Another is President Trump's cruise missile attack on a Syrian airbase early in 2017.

DISCUSSION STARTERS

- Why did a majority of senators decide to acquit Bill Clinton in his Senate trial? Do you agree or disagree with that decision? Why?

- Why did President Nixon decide to resign? Do you think he took the honorable path? Why or why not?

- In your view, was the limit placed on presidential power by the 1973 War Powers Act a good move? Why or why not?

CHAPTER 4

CONGRESS CHECKS THE COURTS

The US Supreme Court Building
is home to the nation's highest court.

The Constitution gives federal judges full authority over the
nation's court system, giving these individuals an enormous
amount of power. But the founders held that the three
branches of government should be equal in stature and
power. There must, therefore, be ways for each branch to
keep the other two from gaining too much power. To prevent
judges from abusing their authority, the founders gave
Congress several anti-judiciary checks.

THE SENATE'S ROLE IN CHOOSING JUDGES

One of those congressional checks on the judiciary involves how federal judges are selected. The president nominates someone to the bench. It is Congress, however, that has the final say. According to the Constitution, the nominee cannot attain that position without the "advice and consent of the Senate."[1] By a two-thirds vote of its members, it either confirms or rejects that nominee. From 1789 to April 2017, various presidents nominated 162 people to the Supreme Court. Of those, 125 were confirmed.

By tradition, when the president offers a nominee, the Senate holds public hearings. The proposed judge faces a panel of senators who ask him or her questions about the law and other matters. The nominee's answers help determine whether the Senate will vote to confirm. That long-standing tradition became the subject of a political controversy in 2016. That February, Supreme Court justice Antonin Scalia died. Soon afterward, President Obama nominated Judge Merrick Garland to the post. Garland looked forward to his confirmation hearings in the Senate.

Those hearings never happened, however. Republican leaders in Congress refused to hold them and also denied

Garland an up-or-down vote. It was an election year, and they hoped a Republican candidate would win the presidency in November. If so, he would have the chance to replace Scalia.

Americans were sharply divided over the Senate's refusal to deal with Garland's nomination. Those who agreed with the Republican leaders cited the Constitution. Nowhere, they said, does it say that senators must hold hearings on judges. Neither does it require them to vote on a nominated judge.

Judge Merrick Garland was nominated by President Barack Obama to fill a Supreme Court vacancy in 2016, but the Senate refused to hold confirmation hearings.

People on the other side of the issue also referred to the Constitution. They pointed to the part that calls for the Senate's "advice and consent" on presidential nominees. They argued that hearings and voting on the nominee are part of the advice and consent process. The Alliance for Justice, which observes and reports on the Supreme Court, took this stance. By refusing to hold "a hearing or vote on" Garland, the Alliance stated, the Senate failed its "constitutional duty."[2]

Eventually this debate became permanently unresolved. Donald Trump won the November 2016 presidential election. It then fell to him to fill Scalia's seat on the high court. In January 2017, he nominated Judge Neil Gorsuch, whom the Senate confirmed in April.

IMPEACHING A JUDGE

Another powerful check Congress can use on the judiciary is impeachment. The House can charge a federal judge with wrongdoing. As in the case of an impeached president, a trial takes place in the Senate. If a minimum of two-thirds of the senators vote to convict, the judge is removed from the bench.

In 1804, for example, the House impeached federal judge John Pickering for drunkenness and making illegal rulings. The Senate convicted him, thereby removing him from the bench. Similarly, in 1873 the House charged federal judge

Mark W. Delahay with drunkenness. In that case, however, he resigned before his Senate trial in order to avoid conviction. Judge Robert Archbald, of Pennsylvania, did not resign and paid a price for it. In 1913, he was impeached, convicted, and removed on a charge of taking bribes.

Another widely publicized impeachment case involving a judge had an unusual final outcome. In August 1988, the House charged Alcee Hastings with bribery and perjury, or lying while under oath. The accused called it "a dark day for myself and the judicial process." He also predicted that the Senate would acquit him.[3] Instead, it convicted him and removed him from the bench. Hastings got the last laugh, however. Less than three years later, in 1992, he was elected as a congressman in Florida. He then took his seat in the very legislative body that had impeached him.

A PANEL OF SENATORS OR THE FULL SENATE?

One federal judge the Senate removed from office challenged his conviction. In 1989, Judge Walter Nixon was impeached for and convicted of perjury. Afterward, he sued the Senate. He argued that the Constitution calls for all the senators to take part in the impeachment trial. In his case, however, a panel of only 12 senators tried him. Nixon appealed to the Supreme Court. He was unhappy, however, when all the justices rejected his argument. The court ruled that the Senate can try impeachment cases in whatever manner it pleases.

TWO NOMINEES?

After President Trump nominated Judge Neil Gorsuch to the Supreme Court, many Democrats were angry. They felt it was unfair that President Trump got the nominee he wanted, whereas President Obama's nominee, Merrick Garland, had been passed over. In late February 2017, Senator Tom Udall of New Mexico suggested an unusual approach to dealing with this problem. Udall publicly stated that he had a way for President Trump to try to unite the country on the issue of Gorsuch and Garland. Why not put both judges on the high court? First, Trump would meet with a Supreme Court justice who was considering retiring soon. Hopefully, Udall explained, that person would be willing to "submit a resignation." Merrick Garland would then become his or her "replacement." Meanwhile, Gorsuch would be confirmed by the Senate as planned. Both men would reach the bench at the same time. "To me," Udall said, that would demonstrate "presidential leadership."[4] Neither Trump nor the Republican senators were willing to go along with such a plan, however. So Gorsuch ended up on the court, and Garland did not.

Senator Tom Udall proposed a unique solution to the Garland-Gorsuch problem.

42

PASSING NEW LEGISLATION

Congress has other ways to check the power of federal judges. The legislature can overturn a court decision by passing a new law. That legislation in a sense cancels out the decision. This congressional ability is not mentioned specifically in the Constitution. Rather, it arises in the course of the regular legislative practices the Constitution allows.

For example, in 1986 the Supreme Court handed down a decision regarding people with disabilities. The case was known as the *Department of Transportation v. Paralyzed Veterans of America*. The court's decision protected the civil rights of people with disabilities in most situations. One exception was in the airline industry. Members of Congress viewed that exception as glaring and unfair. To fix it, they passed a new law—the Air Carrier Access Act. It specifically banned discrimination against people with disabilities who travel by air. In an indirect manner, the new law's passage reversed

A NEW LAW REVERSES FIVE COURT DECISIONS

One of the best-known cases of Congress reversing a Supreme Court decision occurred in 1991. Two years before, the high court had ruled on five separate cases involving civil rights. These decisions were widely seen to promote discrimination because they seemed to restrict the rights of ordinary workers. Led by Senator Edward Kennedy and Congressman Hamilton Fish Jr., many members of Congress agreed and decided to act. Their 1991 legislation made it much easier for workers to fight discrimination. The new law stated that its intention was "to respond to recent decisions of the Supreme Court." The goal, it said, was "to provide adequate protection to victims of discrimination."[5] The bill had to be signed by the president before it could become law. Fortunately for its backers, President George H. W. Bush did sign it. With the stroke of his pen, he allowed Congress to reverse five Supreme Court decisions.

the high court's earlier decision.

A more final and permanent way to overrule a judge's decision is to pass an amendment to the Constitution. Federal judges—even those on the Supreme Court—cannot amend that pivotal document. The founders ensured that only Congress can initiate Constitutional amendments. As with all new laws, judges can review and interpret those amendments. They can point out weaknesses. To date, however, the Supreme Court has never labeled a proposed amendment unconstitutional.

The US founders felt it was important to allow Congress to amend the Constitution. Noted legal scholar Douglas Linder explains that they had two main reasons. "First," he says, they "were under no illusions" that the document they were creating "was perfect." Perhaps "future generations of Americans" would benefit from changes. "Second, they believed that a flexible constitution" would protect the nation from future "upheavals" they could not then predict.[6]

CHANGING THE NUMBER OF JUDGES

Congress can also check or control the powers of federal courts by limiting the number of judges. One way it does this is by deciding how many federal courts will exist at a given moment. This power is provided in Article 3, Section 1, of

The 2017 Supreme Court is one of the most diverse courts ever.

the Constitution. It states that Congress "may from time to time ordain and establish" lower federal courts. Thus, by limiting the number of courts, the legislature can limit the number of sitting judges.

Similarly, Congress can alter the number of Supreme Court justices at any time. Today, nine justices sit on the high court. That has not always been the case, however. In fact, in writing the Constitution, the founders did not specify the number of justices. Congress addressed that matter later. In September 1789, it passed the Judiciary Act. Among other things, it fixed the number of high court justices at six. The act stated, in part, "the Supreme Court of the United States shall consist of a chief justice and five associate justices."[7]

That number was not considered written in stone, so to speak. In the years that followed, Congress occasionally changed it. First, legislators made it seven, then nine, then ten justices. Later still, the number went back down to six, and finally back up to the present nine. Congress was most satisfied with the numbers seven and nine. This is because the court is more productive with an odd number of justices, removing the possibility of a fruitless tie vote.

The upshot of all these anti-judiciary checks is that the federal courts cannot seriously abuse their powers. Congress stands ever ready as a safeguard against that danger.

DISCUSSION STARTERS

- In your view, was the Senate's refusal to give Judge Merrick Garland an up-or-down vote fair? Why or why not?

- The legislative check on the judiciary illustrated in the Air Carrier Access Act decision is not mentioned in the Constitution. Should it be? Explain your answer.

- In your opinion, is Congress's ability to change the number of justices any time it wants a good thing? Why or why not?

CHAPTER 5

CONGRESS CHECKS ITSELF

The framers used the Constitution to outline checks and balances between the houses of Congress, too.

The founders of the country wisely foresaw the necessity for Congress to check the president's powers. They also provided for the legislature to be able to limit the Supreme Court's authority. The Constitution's framers did not stop there, however. They also recognized that the government's third branch might need some oversight and that Congress might well need to check its own powers now and then.

WHEN ONE HOUSE CHECKS THE OTHER

For that reason, the Constitution contains certain legislative checks on Congress. The first and most obvious of these is the division of the national legislature into two separate but coequal houses. Indeed, the framers addressed this major check in the very first section of the Constitution's first article.

Although simple and straightforward, this division of power is highly effective. First, any legislative bill, or proposed law, must pass in both congressional houses in order to go into effect. Thus, if the House passes a bill that is very flawed or unpopular, it does not automatically become a law. That piece of legislation next goes to the Senate. The senators examine and debate the bill. Often they make various changes before passing it. Or they may reject the bill entirely. If that happens, the proposed law might be dead for good, although still another avenue is possible. The Senate can send the bill back to the House. Its members can then rework the legislation and give it to the senators once more. If the Senate likes the revisions and approves them, the bill goes to the president, who signs it into law.

In this way, Congress's two houses can limit each other's powers. Particularly common are instances in which the

Senate simply puts the brakes on an unpopular bill passed by the House. Over the years, that sort of legislative check has occurred thousands of times. One of the more recent examples occurred in 2017. In a vote of 217 to 213, the House voted to dismantle a major piece of existing legislation, the Affordable Care Act (ACA), also known as Obamacare.

The ACA became law in 2010 when Barack Obama was president. A sweeping health care plan, it had been popular with most Democrats and independents. Many Republicans disliked it, however. Congressional Republicans, especially in the House, wanted to repeal it. Among them was Speaker of the House Paul Ryan, the chief officer of the House of Representatives. "A lot of us have been waiting seven years to cast this vote," he said on May 4, 2017. "Many of us are here because we pledged to cast this very vote, to repeal and replace Obamacare."[1]

Ryan and other House Republicans were naturally overjoyed when the bill

Trump and Ryan held a press conference to announce the House's vote to overturn the Affordable Care Act on May 4, 2017.

intended to dismantle the ACA passed. Their enthusiastic mood was short-lived, however. Due to the checks and balances the framers added to the Constitution, the legislation swiftly moved to the Senate. There, the mood surrounding the bill was very different. Within mere hours of the bill's passage in the House, several senators announced they would not vote on it. Instead, they would begin drafting new health care legislation of their own, which would go back to the House for its approval. The Senate thereby rejected the House bill outright. In doing so, the senators exercised a powerful check on their colleagues in the House.

DUTIES, TRANSPARENCY, AND SECRECY

The framers placed another legislative check on Congress by making its work largely transparent. That is, in most cases lawmakers cannot debate and vote in secret. A separate clause of Article 1, Section 5, says that "each house shall keep a Journal of its Proceedings." Furthermore, "from time to time" each house must "publish the same."[2] A more complex version of the original congressional journals developed during the 1800s. Consisting of detailed records of speeches and votes, it is known as the Congressional Record.

The Congressional Record allows the American people to track Congress's normal activities. But on occasion, Congress needs to keep something secret for reasons of national security. Such situations can occur anytime. But they are perhaps most common during wartime. A now well-known example happened during World War II (1939–1945). Early in the conflict, the United States began developing the atomic bomb. At the time totally secret, that project needed the then-enormous sum of $2 billion from Congress to build a site to construct the weapon. President Franklin D. Roosevelt approached Senator Kenneth McKellar of Tennessee.

BIRTH OF THE CONGRESSIONAL RECORD

Article 1, Section 5, Clause 3, of the Constitution calls for the Senate and House to maintain records of their daily actions. That way, the American people can keep a close eye on Congress. At first, however, the records in question were not very detailed. They consisted only of general descriptions of what happened each day in Congress and did not include the full texts of the speeches made by members. In the early 1800s, some major newspapers in New York City and Philadelphia began sending reporters to observe Congress in action. Those individuals wrote down the actual speeches delivered in the House and Senate. Later, in 1873, the Government Printing Office took over this function. It also started publishing the speeches and other information as the Congressional Record. Today, that vital resource is available online at the US Congress's website.

McKellar was then in charge of the Senate appropriations committee, which authorizes Congressional spending to fund various national projects.

The president clearly needed Congress to put up the money to develop the bomb. But it was imperative that the public not know how the money would be spent. So Roosevelt asked McKellar, "Can you hide $2 billion for this super-secret national defense project?" The senator answered, "Well, Mr. President, of course I can. And where in Tennessee did you want me to hide it?"[3] That was McKellar's humorous way of requesting that the new facility be built in his state.

EXPULSION AND CENSURE

Still other legislative checks on Congress allow it to discipline members for bad behavior. These procedures are necessary to ensure that no member abuses the considerable power he or she holds. The most extreme punishment of this type is expulsion. When a member is expelled, he or she is removed from office and must immediately leave Congress.

To expel a member, the Senate or House accuses the person of what the Constitution calls "disorderly behavior."[4] Beyond that, the document mentions no specific acts or charges. The most common charge is that the member has engaged in some sort of corruption or dishonest activity while in office. The Senate or House holds a vote to decide that person's fate. If two-thirds or more of the members present vote yes, he or she is expelled.

Quite often, the accused member chooses to avoid this public humiliation and resigns before the expulsion vote occurs. For example, in 1862 Senator James F. Simmons of Rhode Island was accused of corruption. A committee of senators investigated him. They concluded he was guilty and set a date for his official expulsion vote. Simmons resigned shortly before that day.

Congress can also vote to censure, a

GROUNDS FOR CENSURE IN THE HOUSE

The US Constitution allows the Senate and House to "punish" members for "disorderly behavior." These are very general terms, and the framers did not specify which behaviors should be considered unacceptable. As a result, over time each congressional house developed its own rules about such punishment. The House, for example, decided which kinds of bad behavior would be grounds for censure. Usually, such acts fall under the general term "misconduct."[5] Typical examples are using crude or rude language on the House floor and physically assaulting another member. One noted congressional censure took place in July 1990. The target was Senator David F. Durenberger, a Republican from Minnesota. His colleagues denounced him for failing to report travel expenses and for other financial offenses. They said that in doing so he had dishonored the Senate. Thereafter, Durenberger did not run for reelection.

Jeannette Rankin was a pioneer in the House of Representatives.

less severe method of disciplining a member. In such a case, the person is not forced out of office. Instead, he or she is strongly criticized in a public statement. This embarrassment can negatively affect the member's image. In 2010, for instance, the Senate censured Charles Rangel of New York for raising public funds in an improper manner. He had to stand before the other members while someone read the charges against him aloud. Expulsion and censure remain small but key parts of the checks and balances system the framers fashioned for Congress. That system helps to keep the Senate and House running efficiently and fairly.

The concept of fairness in Congress began to be questioned in another way in the late 1800s and early 1900s. Increasingly, people pointed out the lack of diversity in that body. There were no women in it until Jeannette Rankin of

Wyoming was elected to the House in 1916. Indeed, as late as 1991, the Senate had only two women (Nancy Kassebaum of Kansas and Barbara Mikulski of Maryland). The situation began to improve the following year when four more women entered Congress. By 2017, there were 104 women in Congress, making up about 19 percent of the total of 535 members.

That year actually set a record for diversity in the legislature. Its membership had come to include numerous minorities. Among them were 49 African Americans, 38 Hispanics, 30 Jews, 15 Asians, 7 openly LGBT people, 4 Hindus, 3 Buddhists, and 2 Muslims. One underrepresented group that was still noticeably absent was Native Americans.[6]

DISCUSSION STARTERS

- Some people argue that keeping information secret for security reasons is unnecessary. They hold that the public should know everything that is going on in government at all times, no matter how sensitive. Do you agree or disagree, and why?

- A member of Congress who is about to be expelled can resign before the vote is taken. In your view, is that acceptable or unacceptable behavior? Why?

CHAPTER 6

THE PRESIDENT CHECKS CONGRESS

The checks and balances the Constitution's framers created are many and evenhanded. Just as Congress can check the president's powers, he or she can do the same to the legislature. The use of the words *he or she* here is a formality, to show that it is possible for a woman to be president. In reality, however, so far all US presidents have been men. This lack of gender diversity is widely seen as a weakness in the existing system. Most political experts believe it is only a matter of time before a woman is elected chief executive of the United States.

In 2016, Democrat Hillary Clinton became the first woman to win the presidential nomination of a major party, but she was defeated in the general election by Donald Trump.

The Constitution is mute on this point, however. Whether male or female, the president has the same options to check congressional authority. The best known of these methods is the veto. According to Article 1, Section 7, of the Constitution, the chief executive can veto, or reject, any bill Congress has passed.

The use of such vetoes has been extremely varied. Seven chief executives did not veto a single bill. Most of them—including Thomas Jefferson and John Quincy Adams—were among the earlier US presidents. In contrast, a few leaders vetoed many bills that Congress sent them. Ulysses S. Grant, for example, issued 93 vetoes. Harry S. Truman vetoed 250 bills, and Franklin D. Roosevelt rejected a whopping 635 bills.[1]

On occasion, the specific kinds of bills a president vetoes become an issue for Congress. The best-known example concerns President Andrew Johnson. Several of his 29 vetoes kept Congress from severely punishing Southern states after the Civil War. This angered the legislators so much that they sought reasons to impeach Johnson.

STANDARD VETO VERSUS POCKET VETO

The standard veto is not the only kind of veto with which a president can check congressional power. He or she can also employ the pocket veto. When Congress sends a bill to be signed, the president has ten days to do so. If he or she signs it, it becomes law. Sometimes the president does not sign the bill in those ten days. Usually it becomes law anyway. But if Congress adjourns during that period, the unsigned bill does not

VETO RECORD HOLDERS

Over the centuries, American presidents have used their veto power to check Congress more than 2,500 times. Some were standard vetoes. Others were pocket vetoes. Out of all those vetoes, Congress overrode them only a little more than 100 times. The all-time record holder for vetoes was Franklin D. Roosevelt. He issued 372 standard vetoes and 263 pocket vetoes, for a total of 635. Moreover, Congress overrode him only nine times. A close second was Grover Cleveland. His standard vetoes numbered 346 and his pocket vetoes 238, for a total of 584. A mere seven of these resulted in overrides. Harry S. Truman, who succeeded Roosevelt, racked up 180 standard vetoes and 70 pocket vetoes. Of his total of 250 vetoes, Congress overrode 12. The last of the big four veto issuers was Dwight D. Eisenhower. He rejected 73 bills in the standard manner and 108 as pocket vetoes, for a total of 181. Only two were overridden by Congress. These four presidents issued an amazing 1,650 vetoes. In contrast, all the other presidents combined issued only 924 vetoes.[2]

become law. In that case, the president's inaction constitutes a pocket veto.

In December 2007, George W. Bush provided an example of how this veto option works. At the time, Bush's administration was trying to rebuild war-torn Iraq. Congress passed a bill that exposed the Iraqi government to expensive lawsuits. Bush disliked it, saying that it "would imperil billions of dollars of Iraqi assets."[3] He took advantage of the fact that Congress adjourned right after sending him the bill. For ten days he let the legislation sit, unsigned. As a result, it did not become law.

Why did the framers create the pocket veto? After all, they had already given the president the standard veto to check congressional authority. The answer lies in Congress's ability to adjourn itself. Imagine there were no pocket veto. In that case, the legislature could pass a bill it does not want the president to veto. Right after passing the proposed law, Congress could adjourn for ten or more days and give the president the bill when it returns. Because the chief executive has only ten days to issue a standard veto, it would then be too late for him to keep the bill from becoming law. The pocket veto allows the president to prevent Congress from using this unfair tactic.

Bush's rejection of the Iraq bill in 2007 was his only pocket veto (out of a total of 12 vetoes). Several presidents used many more pocket vetoes than he did. Theodore Roosevelt took that route 40 times, for example. Dwight D. Eisenhower did so 108 times, and Grover Cleveland 238 times. Franklin Roosevelt still holds the record for the use of pocket vetoes, with 263.[4]

Franklin Delano Roosevelt was the president of the United States from 1933 to 1945.

TIEBREAKERS AND SPECIAL SESSIONS

A very different way the president can check congressional power is by using his second in command. The vice president is not merely the person who takes over if the president dies or is incapacitated. The vice president is also an officer of the Senate. Article 1, Section 3, of the Constitution states that he or she is president of that body. Normally, the framers stated, the vice president "shall have no vote." One important exception is when the senators are evenly divided on an issue. In such a case, the vice president can vote and break the tie. It is understood by all that he will vote as his boss, the president, instructs. Therefore, this tie-breaking authority is an executive check on senatorial power.

The president can further control or maneuver Congress by calling that body into a special session. Normally, the House and Senate meet on their own schedules. As part of those timetables, they take recesses, or breaks, from time to time. Article 2, Section 3, of the Constitution gives the president the authority to interrupt such a break. The chief executive can convene one or both congressional houses to deal with whatever he or she sees fit. Moreover, the president can keep the session going as long as needed. The members of the

CIVIL WAR SESSION

On July 4, 1861, President Abraham Lincoln convened a special session of Congress. A few months earlier, in April, most Southern states had seceded from the Union. That marked the start of the bloody Civil War (1861–1865). At first, Lincoln had asked the states to raise 75,000 soldiers to suppress the rebellion. But soon, it became clear that would not be enough. So he called Congress into special session. "Your attention is not called to any ordinary subject of legislation," he told them. Nothing less than an "attempt to destroy the Federal Union" was taking place. Surely some new law would now help to stop the rebellion, he remarked. If so, it "is submitted entirely to the better judgment of Congress." Lincoln requested that the legislators raise at least "400,000 men and $400,000,000." The president said he sincerely hoped "that your views and your action may" match his own. His desire, he explained, was to see a "speedy restoration" of the nation "under the Constitution and the laws." He added that he had chosen that path "with pure purpose. [So] let us renew our trust in God and go forward without fear and with manly hearts."[5] Realizing that the very survival of the nation was at stake, members of Congress gave the president what he asked for.

President Abraham Lincoln called a special session of Congress to build an army to fight the Confederacy in 1861.

TIEBREAKERS

Twelve vice presidents never had to break a tie in the Senate. One was Joseph R. Biden. As President Barack Obama's second in command, Biden served for 2,292 days as vice president. During that interval, no senatorial tie materialized. The experience of Biden's successor, Mike Pence, vice president to Donald Trump, was very different. Only 18 days into the start of his vice presidency, Pence broke his first tie.

House and Senate are therefore forced to deal with the issue at hand. That makes this a very potent use of presidential power over the legislature.

Typically, the president calls a special session for an important reason. For example, the fourth president, James Madison, urgently convened Congress in November 1811. War was looming with Britain, he told those gathered. It was vital that Congress consider preparing US military forces. He recommended "that adequate provisions be made for filling the [army] ranks and prolonging the enlistments of the regular troops."[6] The conflict that ensued became known as the War of 1812 (1812–1815).

Similarly, on September 1, 2005, President George W. Bush called Congress into special session. In this case, Hurricane Katrina had recently devastated the Gulf Coast. It was critical that extra funds be raised for the Federal Emergency Management Agency (FEMA) to deal with the crisis. The leaders of the two congressional houses issued a joint statement.

"The [Bush] administration notified the leadership of the Congress earlier today," it said. FEMA was "running low on funds" and required "immediate assistance."[7]

RECESS APPOINTMENTS

Still another way the US president can check congressional power is through the use of recess appointments. Every chief executive appoints judges, ambassadors, and other high-placed officials. When that happens, Congress regularly exercises its own check on presidential power as the Senate holds hearings and either approves or rejects those appointments. A recess appointment is a presidential counter to that congressional approval process. While Congress is in recess, the president can make an appointment of his or her choice. Because congressional members are on recess, they cannot hold hearings and reject the nominee.

THE HISTORIC HUNDRED DAYS

Perhaps the most memorable of the special sessions of Congress that presidents have called happened in March 1933. Franklin D. Roosevelt convened the legislature immediately after his inauguration. It came in the wake of a national crisis called the Great Depression, the most serious economic downturn in US history. During the historic Hundred Days that followed, the president guided Congress through a spectacular burst of activity. Dozens of emergency bills passed, and the nation was set on a path to recovery.

After viewing the damage from Hurricane Katrina, President George W. Bush called a special session of Congress to provide funding to help address the crisis.

Between 1789 and 2000, US presidents made more than 300 recess appointments. The most controversial of these were ones that filled vacancies on the Supreme Court. In particular, historians and political observers point to three recess appointments made by Dwight D. Eisenhower in the 1950s. These were Supreme Court justices Earl Warren, William J. Brennan, and Potter Stewart. Warren became Chief Justice of the high court. Fortunately for all concerned, these individuals served with distinction.

"Whatever your politics, these are not political hacks," judge and scholar Diana G. Motz points out. "Rather, all [three] seem to have had no trouble maintaining the appropriate judicial independence."[8] The outcomes of executive checks on Congress therefore depend on the skills of the person using those checks. History has shown that thoughtful, sensible presidents tend to use them well.

DISCUSSION STARTERS

- If the pocket veto did not exist, what could Congress do to keep the president from issuing a veto?

- Do you think it is fair for the president to hold the check of the recess appointment over the heads of members of Congress? Why or why not?

- Why do you think it is that making recess appointments to the Supreme Court has always been seen as far more controversial than other kinds of recess appointments?

CHAPTER 7

OTHER PRESIDENTIAL CHECKS

In addition to its constitutional checks on Congress, the executive branch has other ways to limit governmental authority. For instance, the president exerts certain powers over the judiciary branch. One of these checks involves hiring judges. The Constitution provides the president with the power to choose and appoint judges.

As is true with all citizens, some judges are politically conservative, while others are liberal. Still others are moderate. A conservative president is more likely to nominate conservative judges. Similarly, a liberal president

Alexander Hamilton argued in favor of giving the president the power to issue pardons.

usually appoints liberal judges. In this way, a president tends to pick judges who can be expected to make decisions he or she favors. "Politics plays a vital role in how a justice gets his or her job," *Washington Post* reporter Robert Barnes explains. "Presidents look for those with similar views and values."[1]

PRESIDENTIAL HIRING AND FIRING

The president is also able to hire officials within the executive branch and in various departments that the executive branch oversees. This ability is provided for in Article 2, Section 2, of the Constitution. Such officials can be high-ranking members of the cabinet. For example, they might be the secretaries of state and the treasury. Or they can occupy lower-level but still crucial positions, such as the director of the FBI. In addition, they might be generals or other military officers. In hiring these officials, the chief executive exerts a certain amount of control over them. This is because the president tends to look for people who share his or her personal values and beliefs.

Firing officials in or connected to the executive branch is a very different matter. First, the Constitution does not mention such removals as a presidential power. Over the years, various court rulings have attempted but failed to define that power. The accepted opinion of most legal experts is "that there are some purely executive officials who must be removable by the president." Otherwise, he or she would not "be able to accomplish his constitutional role."[2] As a result, presidents have tended to fire political appointees at will, with few challenges.

The reasons for a president's removal of people within the executive branch have varied. More often than not, the president has felt that an official was

HARRY TRUMAN VERSUS DOUGLAS MACARTHUR

Probably the most famous case of a US president firing a military general happened in April 1951. Before that, General Douglas MacArthur led US forces in the Korean War. A talented general, MacArthur kept North Korea from overrunning America's ally, South Korea. However, he and President Harry Truman clashed over many policies and issues, including the role of a civilian president leading the military. Eventually, Truman decided MacArthur had to go. The president explained the firing, saying he needed to eliminate any "confusion as to the real purpose and aim of our policy."[3]

no longer performing his or her job effectively. That reason was certainly common in several cases in which presidents fired military generals. The removal of General George B. McClellan on November 5, 1862, was a famous example. President Abraham Lincoln had earlier hired McClellan to lead the main Union army in the Civil War. McClellan showed himself to be a good troop organizer. But over time Lincoln came to feel he was not aggressive enough as a general. So the president fired him.

Lincoln's removal of McClellan proved highly controversial. No less divisive was President Donald Trump's firing of Sally Yates on January 30, 2017. Yates had recently been serving as acting attorney general in the US Justice Department. On January 27, the president had signed his widely publicized travel ban. It barred people from seven mostly Muslim countries from entering the United States. Trump had expected the Justice Department to help enforce the ban.

To the president's surprise, however, Yates said she would not uphold the ban. In her view, it discriminated against Muslims. Therefore, she said, it went against her department's "solemn obligation to always seek justice and stand for what's right."[4] Trump argued that the ban was needed for national security reasons. In his view, Yates's job was to carry out the president's orders. Because she

In 2017, President Donald Trump fired acting attorney general Sally Yates for her refusal to support his travel ban.

refused to do so, he fired her. The dismissal ignited a firestorm of controversy as Americans proved sharply divided over the issue.

PRESIDENTIAL PARDONS

Another power the president exerts over the judiciary involves pardons. The chief executive can pardon any and all individuals who have been convicted by judges. Moreover, neither Congress nor anyone else can review or reverse presidential pardons. As a result, the pardon has become one of the more touchy and controversial presidential powers.

Several of the founders argued for including pardoning power in the Constitution. They hoped that such pardons might right historic wrongs or ease political tensions. The question was whether to give that pardoning power to Congress or the president. The consensus among the framers was that the chief executive was the best choice. In his Federalist No. 74, Alexander Hamilton made that argument. "One man appears to be a more eligible dispenser of the mercy of the government than a body of men," he wrote. "A single man of prudence and good sense is better fitted" to issue pardons.[5]

Hamilton's colleague, George Washington, agreed fully. While serving as the nation's first president, Washington issued the first presidential pardons in US history. In 1794, a group

President Gerald Ford was heavily criticized for issuing a pardon to Richard Nixon after Nixon's resignation made Ford the president in 1974.

of Pennsylvania whisky distillers grew angry over high taxes on that product. They rioted and burned a tax inspector's house. Worried that the rebellion might spread, Washington led a force of soldiers into Pennsylvania. His men arrested 20 rioters. Of these, two were convicted of treason and sentenced to be hanged. Washington weighed the situation and considered that executing the men might cause further discontent. So in July 1795, he pardoned both of them. Sure enough, peace swiftly returned to the region.

More controversial was a presidential pardon that occurred almost two centuries later. In the early 1970s, President Richard Nixon became involved in the cover-up of a crime. It became known as the Watergate scandal after the name of the building that men loyal to Nixon had burglarized. He denied any guilt. But Congress moved forward to impeach him and remove

TRUMP FIRES COMEY

President Trump's dismissal of Sally Yates in January 2017 caused much controversy. It was not the only news-making firing in his early presidency, however. A little more than three months later, he removed FBI director James Comey. In a letter, Trump told Comey he was "not able to effectively lead" the FBI anymore. This was the official explanation. The problem for Trump was that many people did not believe it. Instead, they pointed to Comey's recent activities. For months he had been conducting a special investigation. Russian computer hackers had interfered during the 2016 presidential election. Their interference may have helped Trump defeat his opponent, Democrat Hillary Clinton. Some Trump associates were suspected of helping the Russians in the process. This had been the subject of Comey's probe. Democrats were therefore upset by Comey's dismissal. Even some Republicans were uneasy. One of them was Senator Richard Burr of North Carolina. He said he was "troubled by" the firing's "timing and reasoning."[6] Meanwhile, Trump denied any wrongdoing.

Former FBI director James Comey is sworn in during a Senate Intelligence Committee hearing on June 8, 2017.

him from office. To avoid that degrading outcome, he resigned the presidency in August 1974.

Although Nixon had left office, that did not mean he was safe from prosecution. As the Watergate investigation continued, he might well have been charged with a crime and sent to prison. Realizing this, his successor, President Gerald Ford, took action. On September 8, 1974, he pardoned Nixon. The pardon covered any crimes the former president had "committed or may have committed" while in office.[7]

Some Americans agreed with Ford's act of mercy. They felt it helped the country to get past the disruptive Watergate scandal. Others strongly disagreed. They argued that the pardon allowed Nixon to get away with his misdeeds. Ford's pardon of his predecessor was therefore hugely controversial. Some observers suspected it contributed to Ford's loss to Jimmy Carter in the 1976 presidential election.

THE TWENTY-FIFTH AMENDMENT

In most cases of hiring and firing within the executive branch, the president exerts control over others. One peculiar exception to that rule exists, providing for the president's own power to be checked by other members of the executive branch. This little-known provision is part of the Constitution's Twenty-Fifth Amendment, created in 1965.

The process outlined in the provision would be set in motion by the vice president. That official would at some point conclude that the president is no longer able to discharge his or her duties, either for physical reasons, including illness, or mental deficiency. The vice president would next inform the cabinet members. If they agreed, they could temporarily remove the president from office. In the meantime, they must let Congress know what had happened. The legislators would then make the final decision whether the president should be permanently removed.

So far, this section of the Twenty-Fifth Amendment has not been invoked. Yet its existence demonstrates the complex levels of checks and balances built into the executive branch.

DISCUSSION STARTERS

- In your opinion, is it wise for a president to appoint Supreme Court justices who share his or her views and values? Why or why not?

- Based on what you know about President Ford's pardon of former president Nixon, do you feel Ford did the right thing? Why or why not?

- In your view, was President Trump justified in firing Sally Yates? Why or why not?

CHAPTER 8

JUDICIAL CHECKS AND BALANCES

Carefully thought-out checks and balances exist among all three branches of the US government. Of all these limits on power, those wielded by the judicial branch are potentially the broadest. For this reason, the highest court of all—the US Supreme Court—has often come under heavy scrutiny. One complaint was that the court's justices were not diverse enough. All of its members, the critics said, have always been white men. The question was whether it was fair that they should make such important decisions for millions of American women and racial minorities. In time, however, the

Sandra Day O'Connor broke the gender barrier as the first female US Supreme Court justice.

court came to be more diverse. In 1967, Thurgood Marshall became the first African-American Supreme Court justice. Later, in 1981, Sandra Day O'Connor became the first woman to sit on the court. By 2017, three of the nine justices were women: Ruth Bader Ginsburg, Sonia Sotomayor, and Elena Kagan.

These and the nation's other federal judges are able to check the authority of the president, Congress, and other governmental agencies. The judges accomplish this through the judicial review process. Judicial review sometimes results in a court declaring actions by agencies of the government unconstitutional. Those actions are thereafter invalid and illegal. In the realm of governmental checks and balances, therefore, the powers of federal judges are sweeping. Judge Alvin Rubin explains that "the courts are vested with the authority to determine the legitimacy of the acts of the executive and the legislative branches of the government." The role of the judiciary can seem "intrusive," especially when "judicial decisions that truly shape American political life . . . are raised as questions of constitutional interpretation." Judge Rubin quotes Alexis de Tocqueville, a French political scientist and historian, who once remarked, "Scarcely any political question arises in the United States that is not resolved, sooner or later, into a judicial question."[1]

ORIGINS OF JUDICIAL REVIEW

Considering the breadth of judges' powers, it may at first seem surprising that the words *judicial review* do not appear in the Constitution. Rather, that document contains a series of clauses describing judicial authority. They consist mainly of general statements that do not deal with specific situations. Most appear in Article 3, Section 2. The first, for example, says that "judicial power shall extend to all cases" that arise "under this Constitution."

DO NOT SHOUT "FIRE" IN A CROWDED THEATER

The federal courts have sometimes used judicial review to check specific sections of the Constitution. They have done so by reinterpreting or refining those sections. For example, the First Amendment allows US citizens freedom of speech. Yet, in some landmark cases the Supreme Court has said that free speech does not apply in all possible situations. One such case was *Schenck v. United States*, in 1919. Charles Schenck, a member of the Socialist Party, was arrested during World War I. He was charged with violating the Espionage Act, which Congress had created in 1917. That law made it illegal to do something that might impair the war effort. Schenck did this by handing out pamphlets. They advocated that Americans should not join the military. He claimed that his arrest violated his right to free speech. The high court disagreed, however. The justices explained that in wartime the government can put a reasonable limit on free speech. In particular, speech that poses a "clear and present danger"[2] to the public must be curbed. The court used the example of shouting "fire" in a crowded theater, clearly a thoughtless, dangerous act.

Also, federal judges' authority covers "the laws of the United States." In addition, judges can try cases involving disputes "between two or more states" or "between citizens of different states."[3]

Among these various judicial powers, an important one is missing. Nowhere does it say that the federal courts can nullify, or strike down, actions that violate the Constitution. That is, the power of judicial review is not spelled out. Therefore, the principle of that vital concept had to be introduced in practice. That required a court case calling for the Supreme Court to establish its regular interpretation of the Constitution.

That case came along in 1803. *Marbury v. Madison* was rooted in the presidency of the second chief executive, John Adams. Just before leaving office, Adams appointed 59 new judges. There was no time to give them their official commission documents, however. The new president, Thomas Jefferson, wanted to appoint his own judges. So he told his secretary of state, James Madison, not to deliver the commissions.

This action upset one of the appointees, William Marbury. He appealed to the Supreme Court. Chief Justice John Marshall explained that body's decision. Marbury did have a right to his commission, but the court could not order Madison to deliver it. The Judiciary Act of 1789 empowered the courts to deliver commissions to judges. However, Marshall and his fellow judges had just reviewed that law. In doing so, they had found parts of it to be unconstitutional, specifically, the part that gave the courts the power to compel judicial commissions. This meant Marbury could not get his commission. More important, the Supreme Court had for the first time reviewed an existing congressional act and declared it unconstitutional. Thereby Marshall and his colleagues established the power of judicial review. The federal courts have used it ever since.

CHECKING PRESIDENTIAL POWER

Marshall and the other judges nullified a congressional law. In this way, they checked the legislature's authority. Over the years, the high court has found numerous

CLINTON IN REHNQUIST'S HANDS

One little-known judicial check on the executive branch is part of the impeachment process. When a president is charged with wrongdoing, he or she is tried in the Senate. The chief justice of the Supreme Court serves as the judge in the trial. For a while, therefore, the president's fate is in the hands of the chief justice. In President Bill Clinton's impeachment trial in 1999, William Rehnquist was chief justice. After Clinton was acquitted, Rehnquist remarked, "I have been impressed by the quality of debate . . . on the entire question of impeachment as provided for in the Constitution."[4]

other laws passed by Congress unconstitutional. Yet limiting congressional power is only one of several ways that judicial review came to be used. The federal courts have also checked the executive branch from time to time.

One of the most famous examples occurred in the early 1970s, during the Watergate crisis. Some evidence pointed to President Nixon's involvement. The federal prosecutor investigating the case searched for more evidence. Before he could find it, however, Nixon fired him.

The new prosecutor ordered the president to release tape recordings made in the White House. There was a chance these tapes contained evidence against Nixon. He did hand over some tapes, but they were heavily edited. Nixon claimed he could do this thanks to the principle of executive privilege. It allows a sitting president a right to keep certain secrets. The prosecutor disagreed and appealed to the Supreme Court. The justices reviewed the evidence and ruled against the president. They rejected his claim of executive privilege, saying it was unconstitutional. That claim, they stated, "must yield to" the "specific need for evidence in a pending criminal trial."[5] Thus, Nixon had to hand over the full recordings. This eventually led to his downfall.

President-elect George W. Bush, *left*, meets with Al Gore on December 19, 2000, one week after the Supreme Court stopped a recount in Florida and gave Bush the presidency.

OVERRULING LOWER COURTS

The federal courts do much more than check acts by Congress and the president. They also regularly use judicial review to overturn, and thereby check, decisions made by lower courts. A prominent example was the case of *Bush v. Gore*. On Election Day in 2000, George W. Bush led his opponent, Al Gore, in Florida. The difference—approximately 1,800 votes—was small enough to trigger a recount. In the days that followed, the Florida race tightened. Soon Bush led by only 327 votes out of almost six million cast.[6]

At this point, arguments erupted over whether the recount should continue. Gore insisted that it should, and the Florida Supreme Court ruled in his favor. Bush's lawyers then appealed to the US Supreme Court. On December 12, 2000, the justices announced their decision. In a 5-to-4 vote, they said that the Florida Supreme Court's decision was unconstitutional. As a result, the recount stopped, and Bush became president.

In another famous case, the Supreme Court overruled one of its own earlier decisions. The initial case, known as *Plessy v. Ferguson*, took place in 1896. An African-American man named Homer Plessy was arrested for riding in a train car reserved for white people. It was then against the law in some states for the two races to mix that way. He appealed to the Supreme Court, arguing against the separation of the races. The justices rejected his plea, however. In so doing, they firmly established the racist policy of "separate but equal."

THE ISSUE OF PRAYER IN SCHOOL

Some other cases of judicial review in the federal courts have dealt with freedom of religion. One of the more famous examples is *Engel v. Vitale.* In the late 1950s, New York State introduced a prayer into public schools. A parent reacted by suing his child's school. In the Supreme Court in 1962, he argued that saying the prayer in class forced the students to accept a certain religion. The court agreed. It ruled that the prayer violated the Constitution, which grants complete religious freedom.

Thanks to that ruling, racial discrimination continued. By the 1950s, however, many Americans had come to see how unjust this was. Moreover, as society changed, the courts did, too. In the landmark 1954 case *Brown v. Board of Education*, all nine high court justices agreed. They struck down *Plessy v. Ferguson*, labeling it unconstitutional. At the same time, they called racially segregated schools unequal. "In the field of public education," they stated, the rule of "separate but equal has no place."[7] Although the ruling related only to segregation in schools, it proved to be the first step in eliminating segregation everywhere in society. This and other examples of judicial review have repeatedly demonstrated the broad powers of the federal courts. Their influence on American government and society is nothing less than huge.

DISCUSSION STARTERS

- Is it fair and just for a handful of federal court judges to wield such sweeping powers over society? Why or why not?

- Do you think the Supreme Court was justified in ruling on school segregation in 1954? Why or why not?

- In 1962, the Supreme Court ruled that prayer in public schools violated the Constitution. Do you agree? Why or why not?

CHAPTER 9

OTHER CHECKS AND BALANCES

President George W. Bush addresses US troops in Baghdad, Iraq, in 2008. The Constitution dictates that the president is the commander in chief of the military.

The system of checks and balances created by the founders has endured to the present. This is partly evident in the interactions among the federal government's three branches. Each limits the powers of the other two in both bold and subtle ways.

As elegant as that system is, however, the framers went even further. The Constitution also contains a number of other clever and effective checks and balances. Some limit the powers of individual states. In contrast, others allow the states to check the federal government's authority. One even allows civilians—non-military personnel—to check and control the military's considerable powers.

FEDERAL CHECKS ON THE STATES

The powers of the states were certainly on the framers' minds when they wrote the Constitution. After all, the nation was originally composed of a union of 13 states. Each was unique and took pride in its customs and rights. There was therefore much debate about how much power to allow the states. Clearly, the federal government should be able to limit some state powers. Conversely, the states should be able to check some federal authority. The relationship between these state and federal powers is often called federalism.

In those initial arguments about federalism, supporters of federal dominance took a slim lead. Their success can be seen in Article 1, Section 10, of the Constitution. It lists

THE RIGHT OF STATES TO SUE

One of the checks the states can wield against the federal government is the right to sue that government in court. This does not happen often. But when it does, it makes headlines. This was the case in 2016, when Texas, Arizona, and several other states brought such suits. The issue was President Barack Obama's policy of allowing transgender students to use the bathrooms of their choice at school. The states' suits became moot a few months later, however. The next president, Donald Trump, reversed the Obama policy on transgender rights.

many ways in which the federal government can check state powers. For example, it says that no state can sign a treaty with a foreign country. That authority is instead given to the president and Congress: the president negotiates the treaty, and Congress approves it. Similarly, no state can make its own money. That power is reserved to the federal government. Neither can the states collect taxes on foreign imports and exports. Only Congress can do that.

Article 1, Section 10, also says that no state can raise its own army or construct warships to combat a foreign foe in peacetime. The one exception allowed is if a state is directly invaded. The framers understood, however, that such a situation was highly unlikely. If a state was invaded by a foreign nation, the president would surely employ the national army to defend that state.

Another federal check on state powers appears in Article 6. It declares that federal laws outweigh state laws. This part of the Constitution is called the supremacy clause. It says that the federal Constitution is the highest authority in the nation. Thus, says Donald A. Ritchie, "state courts rule on state laws." But, he continues, "the federal courts can step in and order changes if the state laws go against federal law."[1]

THE POWER TO CHANGE THE CONSTITUTION

The states also can limit the federal government's authority. For example, Article 5 of the Constitution explains how the national legislature can propose amendments to the document. If two-thirds of both houses approve, an amendment goes to the states.

First, the state legislatures debate the suggested change. Each decides whether to approve it. In order to be ratified, the amendment must gain the approval of three-fourths of the states. Today that is 38 of the 50 states. Thus, the states hold a lot of power over Congress in the amendment process.

One of those amendments provides an important check on the executive branch. The Twenty-Second Amendment limits the number of four-year terms a president can serve to two terms. The only chief executive to serve more than two terms was Franklin Roosevelt. A Democrat, he was first elected president in 1932. He then went on to win re-elections in 1936, 1940, and 1944. Only months after his fourth inauguration, he died. His vice president, Harry Truman, finished the term. The next Republican-controlled Congress wanted to keep this from happening again. So it ushered through the Twenty-Second Amendment, and the states ratified it in 1951.

CONTROL OF THE MILITARY

The president holds another unique and important power. According to Article 2, Section 2, the president commands the US military. Crucially, the chief executive is a civilian, not a member of the military. In fact, the main military command structure is composed of civilians. Directly under the president is the secretary of defense, for example. He or she is also a civilian. Similarly, if the president can no longer serve, yet another civilian—the vice president—takes his or her place.

Once more, the foresight of the founders is evident. Giving ultimate control of the military to civilians was a safeguard against military dictatorship. Scholar Andrew A. Hill explains "the founders' fear of an unchecked military." This worry, he says, was reflected in "their personal experience." These men

HOW DID ROOSEVELT WIN FOUR TERMS?

Franklin D. Roosevelt served four terms as US president. That set a record unmatched before or since. Roosevelt managed this unusual feat partly because he was a capable leader. Another factor was the unique series of events surrounding him. In 1932, the people elected him to fight the Great Depression's crippling effects. In 1936, the country appeared to be recovering. So the people elected him again. He won again in 1940 with the nation on the verge of World War II. Finally, his 1944 election was partly due to fear of changing leaders in the middle of a war.

Franklin D. Roosevelt is the only president to have been reelected three times.

had suffered "abuse at the hands of the British" soldiers during the American Revolution.[2]

The founders also possessed a wide knowledge of history. They saw numerous past examples of military generals overstepping their authority and becoming tyrants. James Madison commented on this in 1787, while writing the Constitution. "In time of actual war," he said, governments tend to give enormous powers to "the executive." There is danger, he continued, when "the head" grows "too large for the body." By that, he meant that powerful military leaders often abuse their great authority. He added that an army "with an overgrown executive will not long be safe companions to liberty."[3]

One way to check this military threat was to give control of the army to civilians. This explains the framers' adoption of civilian military leaders in Article 2, Section 2. History has shown the wisdom of this move. Throughout the nation's history, the US military has never attempted to control the government. As a result, Hill says, "Americans' historical fears of a too-powerful military have faded."[4]

This is only one of many examples of how well the framers' system of checks and balances has worked in practice. For more than two centuries, it has increasingly made the federal government more responsive to the people's needs and wants. The checks and balances have also made it very difficult for a single person to seize power and become a dictator. Finally, they have repeatedly righted past social wrongs. In so doing, the checks and balances have made life for American citizens fairer, safer, and more just. That process will surely continue, as each new generation reaps the benefits of one of history's great legal documents—the US Constitution.

DISCUSSION STARTERS

- The Constitution says the states cannot raise their own armies. Do you think the states should have the right to create their own armies and use them in wartime separately from the US Army? Why or why not?

- Do you feel that President Obama was right to advocate allowing transgender students to use the school bathrooms of their choice? Why or why not?

TIMELINE

1776

The country's founders issue the Declaration of Independence, announcing the formation of a new nation, the United States of America.

1787

The founders write the US Constitution. They include numerous checks and balances to ensure that no single branch of government can overpower the others.

1803

The court case known as *Marbury v. Madison* provides the Supreme Court an opportunity to establish the crucial practice of judicial review.

1862

In a controversial move during the Civil War, President Abraham Lincoln fires General George B. McClellan.

1868

Congress impeaches President Andrew Johnson. He is tried in the Senate and eventually acquitted.

1873

The Government Printing Office begins publishing the Congressional Record, which distributes all the speeches made and votes taken in Congress.

1913

A federal judge, Robert Archbald, is impeached for taking bribes. He is convicted and removed from the bench.

1919

In *Schenck v. United States*, the Supreme Court says that it is reasonable for the government to place certain limits on free speech in wartime.

1944

President Franklin D. Roosevelt is reelected to a record fourth term. Soon afterward, Congress creates a constitutional amendment that limits presidents to two terms.

1954

In *Brown v. Board of Education*, the Supreme Court finds that segregated schools are unequal and unconstitutional.

1973

Congress passes the War Powers Act, limiting the war-making powers of presidents.

1974

President Richard Nixon resigns the presidency after learning that Congress is about to impeach him for his role in the Watergate scandal. Later that year, President Gerald Ford pardons Nixon.

1990

The Senate issues a censure to David F. Durenberger, a Republican from Minnesota, for not reporting travel expenses and other financial offenses.

2000

In the case of *Bush v. Gore*, the Supreme Court overturns a decision by the Florida Supreme Court that allowed a recount in the presidential election. As a result, George W. Bush wins the election and becomes president.

2005

President George W. Bush calls a special session of Congress to deal with the disastrous effects of Hurricane Katrina.

2010

The House of Representatives censures Congressman Charles Rangel, a Democrat from New York, for ethics violations.

2016

Supreme Court justice Antonin Scalia dies. President Barack Obama chooses Judge Merrick Garland to fill that position, but the Senate refuses to consider Garland's nomination.

2017

President Donald Trump issues a travel ban on people entering the United States from seven mostly Muslim nations. A federal court temporarily blocks the ban.

ESSENTIAL FACTS

MAJOR EVENTS

- In 1787, the founders created the US Constitution, making sure to include a number of checks and balances. These keep the three branches of the central government—the executive, legislative, and judiciary—from overshadowing one another. Some other checks and balances allow the federal government to rein in the states and the states to push back.

- In 1803, the US Supreme Court made a historical and legal precedent in the case known as *Marbury v. Madison*. For the first time, the court reviewed a congressional act and declared it unconstitutional. This case set the precedent for judicial review, a procedure in which the Supreme Court checks the other two branches of government.

- The power of the congressional check of impeachment was shown in 1974. Two years before, a burglary had taken place in the Watergate Building in Washington, DC. Burglars were arrested for attempting to steal Democratic Party documents. The burglary was connected to President Richard Nixon's reelection campaign. Over time, Nixon himself was tied to a cover-up of the crime, and Congress began preparing to impeach him. The mere threat of impeachment convinced Nixon he must resign his office, which he did on August 8, 1974.

- The federal courts have demonstrated their power over presidents numerous times. One of the most dramatic occurred early in 2017. On January 27, President Donald Trump issued a travel ban to keep people from seven Middle Eastern and African nations from traveling to the United States. The purpose, he claimed, was to stop terrorists from entering America. In the months that followed, several federal judges ruled that the ban was unconstitutional. They said it discriminated against Muslims, who make up the majority of the populations of the seven countries.

KEY PLAYERS

THE EXECUTIVE BRANCH OF GOVERNMENT

The executive branch is headed by the president, who serves a four-year term. The president ensures that the laws passed by Congress are carried out.

THE LEGISLATIVE BRANCH OF GOVERNMENT

The legislative branch is composed of the two houses of Congress—the Senate and the House of Representatives (usually called simply "the House"). These bodies suggest, debate, and vote on laws and then send them to the president to sign into law.

THE JUDICIAL BRANCH OF GOVERNMENT

The judicial branch is made up of the US court system. The most powerful courts are the federal ones, headed by the Supreme Court. It has nine justices, who are appointed by the president and serve for life.

IMPACT ON SOCIETY

The checks and balances established in the Constitution by the founders have prevented any one of the three branches of government from becoming tyrannical. Presidential vetoes have stopped unpopular congressional bills from becoming laws. When presidents have vetoed popular bills, Congress has overridden those vetoes. Moreover, the federal courts often check, or limit, the powers of the president and Congress. If one of those two branches acts in a manner that goes against the Constitution and might harm the people, the Supreme Court stops it.

QUOTE

"If men were angels, no government would be necessary. If angels were to govern men, neither external nor internal controls on government would be necessary."

—James Madison, father of the Constitution

GLOSSARY

APPROPRIATION
Money raised by Congress to fund some kind of government project.

CENSURE
A process used by Congress to punish one of its members, whose misdeed is announced in public.

CHECKS AND BALANCES
Safeguards built into the Constitution to keep one branch from overpowering the others.

CIVIL RIGHTS
A guarantee of equal social opportunities and equal protection under the law, regardless of gender, race, religion, or other personal traits.

CIVILIAN
A person not serving in the armed forces.

CONGRESSIONAL RECORD
A massive ongoing collection of all speeches, votes, and other business of the US Congress.

DISCRIMINATION
Unfair treatment of other people, usually because of race, age, or gender.

EXECUTIVE BRANCH
The branch of the US government headed and overseen by the president.

EXPULSION
A process used by Congress to punish one of its members, who is tried for some misdeed and, if convicted, is removed from office.

IMPEACHMENT
A process used by Congress to charge a president, cabinet member, or judge with criminal activity.

JUDICIAL BRANCH
The branch of the US government made up of the federal courts, including the Supreme Court.

JUDICIAL REVIEW
The process by which the federal courts decide whether a law or other act is constitutional or unconstitutional.

LEGISLATION
Bills, or proposed laws, created by Congress.

LEGISLATIVE BRANCH
The branch of the US government made up of the two houses of Congress, the Senate and the House of Representatives.

PRESIDENT-ELECT
A person who has won a presidential election in November and must wait until the following January to be sworn in as president.

RATIFY
To formally approve or adopt an idea or document.

RECESS APPOINTMENT
The process by which a president can appoint a cabinet member or other official while Congress is in recess.

TYRANNY
Cruel and oppressive government rule.

VETO
A check that a president can use against Congress, in which he or she rejects a proposed law submitted by the legislature.

ADDITIONAL RESOURCES

SELECTED BIBLIOGRAPHY

Barron, David J. *Waging War: The Clash between Presidents and Congress, 1776 to ISIS.* New York: Simon, 2016. Print.

Daschle, Tom, and Charles Robbins. *The US Senate: Fundamentals of American Government.* New York: Thomas Dunne, 2013. Print.

Ricar, Sondra. *Checks and Balances: An Introduction to American Government.* El Cajon, CA: National Social Sciences, 2013. Print.

FURTHER READINGS

Brannen, Daniel E. *Checks and Balances: The Three Branches of the American Government.* Detroit: Thomson/Gale, 2005. Print.

Perritano, John. *American Government: Foundations.* Costa Mesa, CA: Saddleback, 2016. Print.

ONLINE RESOURCES

Booklinks
NONFICTION NETWORK
FREE! ONLINE NONFICTION RESOURCES

To learn more about governmental checks and balances, visit **abdobooklinks.com.** These links are routinely monitored and updated to provide the most current information available.

MORE INFORMATION

For more information on this subject, contact or visit the following organizations:

INDEPENDENCE HALL

6th and Market Streets
Philadelphia, PA 19106
215-965-2305

nps.gov/inde

Independence Hall is the site at which the founders met to create the US Constitution. There, at the Constitutional Convention, James Madison and his colleagues added the checks and balances to the historic document.

UNITED STATES CAPITOL

East Capitol Street NE and First Street SE
Washington, DC 20004
202-226-8000

visitthecapitol.gov

The Capitol is not only a great historic structure symbolizing the nation. It is also the place where the US Congress continues to meet each year and pass new laws.

UNITED STATES SUPREME COURT

One First Street, NE
Washington, DC 20543
202-479-3000

supremecourtus.gov

Situated near the US Capitol building, the Supreme Court building is one of the most magnificent pieces of architecture in the country. Each year, the high court's nine justices hear cases and interpret the US Constitution.

SOURCE NOTES

CHAPTER 1. CONGRESS VERSUS ANDREW JOHNSON

1. Andrew Glass. "House Votes to Impeach Andrew Johnson, February 24, 1868." *Politico*. Politico, 24 Feb. 2015. Web. 22 Sept. 2017.

2. Peter Carlson. "Thaddeus Stevens." *HistoryNet*. HistoryNet, 19 Feb. 2013. Web. 22 Sept. 2017.

3. Chester G. Hearn. *The Impeachment of Andrew Johnson*. Jefferson, NC: McFarland, 2000. Print. 170–171.

4. "The Impeachment of Andrew Johnson (1868)." *United States Senate*. US Senate, n.d. Web. 22 Sept. 2017.

5. Hans L. Trefousse. *Andrew Johnson: A Biography*. New York: Norton, 1989. Print. 327.

6. Ibid. 333.

7. LeRoy P. Graf et al, eds. *The Papers of Andrew Johnson, Vol. 14*. Knoxville, TN: University of Tennessee, 2000. Print. 89.

8. Ibid.

9. "The Impeachment of Andrew Johnson (1868)." *United States Senate*. US Senate, n.d. Web. 22 Sept. 2017.

CHAPTER 2. CREATING CHECKS AND BALANCES

1. "Separation of Powers with Checks and Balances." *Documents of Freedom*. Bill of Rights Institute, 2017. Web. 22 Sept. 2017.

2. James Madison. "The Federalist No. 47." *The Federalist Papers*. Alexander Hamilton et al. New York: Bantam, 2003. Print. 292–293.

3. Maura Dolan and Jaweed Kaleem. "'See You in Court,'" Trump Tweets After 9th Circuit Panel Unanimously Refuses to Reinstate His Travel Ban." *Los Angeles Times*. Los Angles Times, 9 Feb. 2017. Web. 22 Sept. 2017.

4. James Madison. "The Federalist No. 51." *The Federalist Papers*. Alexander Hamilton et al. New York: Bantam, 2003. Print. 316.

5. Ibid. 314–316.

6. Ibid.

7. "Bush Vetoes Water Bill; Override Likely." *USA Today*. USA Today, 2 Nov. 2007. Web. 22 Sept. 2017.

CHAPTER 3. CONGRESS CHECKS THE PRESIDENT

1. Chris Edelson. "Limiting Presidential Power." *Baltimore Sun*. Baltimore Sun, 12 July 2016. Web. 22 Sept. 2017.

2. "US Constitution, Article 1, Section 3." *US Constitution*. US Constitution, n.d. Web. 22 Sept. 2017.

3. "President Nixon's Resignation Speech, August 8, 1974." *PBS*. PBS, n.d. Web. 22 Sept. 2017.

4. "Vetoes." *United States Senate*. US Senate, n.d. Web. 22 Sept. 2017.

5. Donald A. Ritchie. *Our Constitution*. New York: Oxford UP, 2006. Print. 89.

6. "US Constitution, Article 2, Section 2." *US Constitution*. US Constitution, n.d. Web. 22 Sept. 2017.

7. Donald A. Ritchie. *The US Congress: A Very Short Introduction*. New York: Oxford UP, 2010. Print. 98.

8. Thomas Patterson. *We the People*. New York: McGraw-Hill, 2015. Print. 442–443.

CHAPTER 4. CONGRESS CHECKS THE COURTS

1. "US Constitution, Article 2, Section 2." *US Constitution*. US Constitution, n.d. Web. 22 Sept. 2017.

2. "Myths vs. Facts on Filling the Supreme Court Vacancy." *Alliance for Justice*. Alliance for Justice, n.d. Web. 22 Sept. 2017.

3. "House Votes to Impeach US Judge." *Los Angeles Times*. Los Angeles Times, 3 Aug. 1988. Web. 22 Sept. 2017.

4. Sean Sullivan. "Why Not Neil Gorsuch and Merrick Garland on the Supreme Court? Senator Floats Long-Shot Plan." *Chicago Tribune*. Chicago Tribune, 27 Feb. 2017. Web. 22 Sept. 2017.

5. Leon Friedman. "Overruling the Court." *American Prospect*. American Prospect, 19 Dec. 2001. Web. 22 Sept. 2017.

6. Douglas Linder. "What in the Constitution Cannot Be Amended?" *School of Law*. University of Missouri-Kansas City, n.d. Web. 22 Sept. 2017.

7. "Judiciary Act: September 24, 1789." *Avalon Project*. Yale Law School, 2008. Web. 22 Sept. 2017.

CHAPTER 5. CONGRESS CHECKS ITSELF

1. Robert King. "House Passes Obamacare Repeal Bill in Cliffhanger 217–213 Vote." *Washington Examiner*. Washington Examiner, 4 May 2017. Web. 22 Sept. 2017.

2. "US Constitution, Article 1, Section 5, Clause 3." *US Constitution*. US Constitution, n.d. Web. 22 Sept. 2017.

3. Cynthia C. Kelly, ed. *Remembering the Manhattan Project*. Hackensack, NJ: World Scientific, 2004. Print. 6–7.

4. "US Constitution, Article 1, Section 5, Clause 2." *US Constitution*. US Constitution, n.d. Web. 22 Sept. 2017.

5. Jack Maskell. "Expulsion, Censure, Reprimand, and Fine: Legislative Discipline in the House of Representatives." *CRS Report for Congress*. US House of Representatives Committee on Rules, 25 Jan. 2005. Web. 22 Sept. 2017.

6. Christina Marcos. "115th Congress Will Be Most Racially Diverse in History." *Hill*. Capitol Hill, 17 Nov. 2016. Web. 22 Sept. 2017.

SOURCE NOTES CONTINUED

CHAPTER 6. THE PRESIDENT CHECKS CONGRESS

1. Donald A. Ritchie. *Our Constitution*. New York: Oxford UP, 2006. Print. 89.

2. John T. Woolley and Gerhard Peters. "Presidential Vetoes." *American Presidency Project*. American Presidency Project, 28 Sept. 2016. Web. 22 Sept. 2017.

3. "Bush to Reject Defense Bill with 'Pocket Veto.'" *NBC News*. NBC News, 28 Dec. 2007. Web. 22 Sept. 2017.

4. John T. Woolley and Gerhard Peters. "Presidential Vetoes." *American Presidency Project*. American Presidency Project, 28 Sept. 2016. Web. 22 Sept. 2017.

5. Abraham Lincoln. "Special Session Message: July 4, 1861." *American Presidency Project*. American Presidency Project, 2017. Web. 22 Sept. 2017.

6. James Madison. "Third Annual Message: November 11, 1811." *American Presidency Project*. American Presidency Project, 2017. Web. 22 Sept. 2017.

7. Richard E. Cohen and John Stanton. "Congress to Hold Special Session on Katrina Relief." *Government Executive*. National Journal Group, 1 Sept. 2005. Web. 22 Sept. 2017.

8. Tim Arnold. "Recess Appointments Both Accepted, Controversial." *UVA Lawyer*. University of Virginia School of Law, Spring 2011. Web. 22 Sept. 2017.

CHAPTER 7. OTHER PRESIDENTIAL CHECKS

1. Robert Barnes. "Justices Tend to Agree with Presidents That Pick Them—But Stray Later." *Washington Post*. Washington Post, 20 Dec. 2015. Web. 22 Sept. 2017.

2. "Annotation 14: Article II." *FindLaw*. FindLaw, 31 May 2017. Web. 22 Sept. 2017.

3. "1951—Truman Relieves MacArthur of Duties in Korea." *History*. A&E Television, 2017. Web. 22 Sept. 2017.

4. Evan Perez and Jeremy Diamond. "Trump Fires Acting AG after She Declines to Defend Travel Ban." *CNN*. CNN, 31 Jan. 2017. Web. 22 Sept. 2017.

5. Alexander Hamilton. "The Federalist No. 74." *The Federalist Papers*. Alexander Hamilton et al. New York: Bantam, 2003. Print. 453–454.

6. Stephen Collinson, Jeff Zeleny, and Jeremy Diamond. "Trump Fires FBI Director James Comey." *CNN*. CNN, 10 May 2017. Web. 22 Sept. 2017.

7. Evans Andrews. "7 Famous Presidential Pardons." *History*. A&E Television, 23 July 2013. Web. 22 Sept. 2017.

CHAPTER 8. JUDICIAL CHECKS AND BALANCES

1. Alvin B. Rubin. "Judicial Review in the United States." *Louisiana Law Review* 40.1(1979): 67. *LSU Law Digital Commons*. Web. 10 Oct. 2017.

2. "*Schenck v. United States.*" *Legal Information Institute*. Cornell Law School, n.d. Web. 10 Oct. 2017.

3. "US Constitution, Article 3, Section 2." *US Constitution*. US Constitution, n.d. Web. 22 Sept. 2017.

4. Richard W. Stevenson. "The President's Acquittal: The Chief Justice; Rehnquist Goes With the Senate Flow, 'Wiser, but Not a Sadder Man.'" *New York Times*. New York Times Company, 13 Feb. 1999. Web. 22 Sept. 2017.

5. "United States v. Nixon." *Nolo*. Nolo, 2017. 22 Sept. 2017.

6. Alex McBride. "Landmark Cases: Bush v. Gore (2000)." *PBS*. Educational Broadcasting, 2007. Web. 22 Sept. 2017.

7. Richard Wormser. "Brown v. Board of Education." *PBS*. Educational Broadcasting, 2002. Web. 22 Sept. 2017.

CHAPTER 9. OTHER CHECKS AND BALANCES

1. Donald A. Ritchie. *Our Constitution*. New York: Oxford UP, 2006. Print. 136–137.

2. Andrew A. Hill, Leonard Wang, and Stephen J. Gerras. "'Self-Interest Well Understood': The Origins and Lessons of Public Confidence in the Military." *School of Strategic Landpower*. US Army War College, n.d. Web. 22 Sept. 2017.

3. Ibid.

4. Ibid.

INDEX

ABOUT THE AUTHOR

DUCHESS HARRIS, JD, PHD

Professor Harris is the chair of the American Studies Department at Macalester College. The author and coauthor of four books (*Hidden Human Computers: The Black Women of NASA* and *Black Lives Matter* with Sue Bradford Edwards, *Racially Writing the Republic: Racists, Race Rebels, and Transformations of American Identity* with Bruce Baum, and *Black Feminist Politics from Kennedy to Clinton/Obama*), she has been an associate editor for *Litigation News*, the American Bar Association Section's quarterly flagship publication, and was the first editor-in-chief of *Law Raza Journal*, an interactive online race and the law journal for William Mitchell College of Law.

She has earned a PhD in American Studies from the University of Minnesota and a Juris Doctorate from William Mitchell College of Law.